AT THE EDGE

ALSO BY GAIL MORAN SLATER

Bare Rooms (chapbook)

AT THE EDGE

Poems by

Gail Moran Slater

Antrim House
Bloomfield, Connecticut

Library of Congress Control Number: 2023900849

ISBN: 979-8-9865522-5-5

First Edition, 2023

Book design by Rennie McQuilkin

Front Cover Image:
Edward Hopper American, 1882 - 1967
Automat, 1927
Oil on canvas, 27 1/8 × 35 in. (71.4 × 88.9 cm)
Des Moines Art Center Permanent Collections;
Purchased with funds from the Edmundson Art
Foundation, Inc., 1958.2
Photo Credit: Rich Sanders, Des Moines

Author photograph by Portrait Simple

Antrim House
860.519.1804
AntrimHouseBooks@gmail.com
www.AntrimHouseBooks.com
400 Seabury Dr., #5196, Bloomfield, CT 06002

Dedicated to my daughter
Julie Slater Flanagan

Nothing compares to you.

INTRODUCTION

The first time a poem showed up on my writing pad was the day of the Winter Solstice, 1997. As one of the poems in this collection attests, I like the light at that time of day and was watching the sun fade behind gray-black leafless poplars. The Sun's retirement at that astronomical moment was commemorated in these lines:

> *Sun is reluctant to retire today*
> *while he can still make a contribution,*
> *but Rules are Rules, and at 4:26 PM*
> *Sun will sever his ties to Earth, Inc.*
> *so younger stars can climb.*

The narrative goes on for four stanzas that I spoke one night at an open mic reading, friends telling me they were entertained. The irony had worked. I submitted the poem to an online contest, *Poems about the Weather.* I won a cash prize of $50 and kept on writing.

Poems don't often materialize like that. In an interview before he died, Seamus Heaney said, "When they do, you have to get out of the way." The little jump-start on that Solstice eve began for me another kind of life wherein I learned a new language. Poetry has come to me from listening to, speaking, reading, and writing its enchantments. My verses have arrived from hours filling up notebooks with lines, tropes, and word choices wherein a real poem takes shape and deserves to be shared. For company on this journey, I have come to know wonderful people who live the poetry life and love the art as I do.

Because my home is just south of Boston/Cambridge, finding other poets at readings or in poetry classes is a snap. We talk about our work, share in formal workshops, criticize, and encourage. Two fine poetry teachers I've known for 10 years have made all the difference in my writing, Katia Kapovich and Tom Daley. They have given classes at the Cambridge Center for Adult Education and the Boston Center for Adult Education respectively, and I am grateful to both of them for their wisdom and experience. Some of my growth in poetry, I'm convinced, comes from returning to the same workshops year by year; I have come to know other writers' oeuvres and celebrated their successes.

Poetry has been the impetus for me to travel in the U.S. and abroad for summer school programs. In Sligo, Ireland, I attended a first-rate workshop led by the poet Justin Quinn, who has published in the *New Yorker* and was enthusiastic about the few pieces I turned out during those heady days. We correspond on social media. Later, I won a bursary (scholarship) to the John Hewitt Summer School in Armagh, Northern Ireland, and was fortunate to meet there a young Scottish professor named Niall Campbell, a prize-winning poet. I've returned often to the notes I took from his kindly observations.

Through contacts I've made in Ireland, I attended a long weekend of reading and writing poems sponsored by The United Irish Cultural Center of San Francisco. I've also attended sessions at Poets House on the West Side of Manhattan, where teachers are trained to inspire a love of poetry in their students, lessons I have brought back to my adult ESL classes. For many of the lonely immigrants I teach, poetry is a place to express feelings, something of an indulgence for a group often focused only on surviving in their new country. My students do well with form poems—cinquains and haiku—and they love displaying their work on classroom bulletin boards. For my classes I've chosen English-language poems by writers whose names indicate cultures the students may identify with, e.g., Ocean Vuong, Naomi Shihab Nye, and William Carlos Williams, among others. We have poetry to thank for the improvements some students have made on State-required post-tests

Every morning I start the day with reading and writing poems. My taste has evolved, and knowing people whose daily lives include the art has opened to me gift after gift of new works and new writers. In my hometown of Hingham, I've been lucky to be part of a group called Living by Heart, where we get together to "say" lines we have fallen for and memorized. Among many poems I know by heart, three stand out. My teacher Tom Daley says they are the only perfect villanelles in the English language: "Do Not Go Gentle into That Good Night" by Dylan Thomas; "One Art" by Elizabeth Bishop; and "The Waking" by

Theodore Roethke. It's wonderful to have lines from those poems at the ready when I am stressed out in the dentist's chair.

Over the years, I've acquired knowledge about how poems live and breathe, their cadence and structure. Even so, what I most want when I read a poem is *heart*. My students' poems often get there, as does the work of some of my friends, but it's in the reading of the greats, poets like Sappho, Dickinson, and Whitman that I find regular satisfaction. As W. B. Yeats wrote in his most popular poem while he was living in London and missing his boyhood home in Sligo, it all came back to him one day "in the deep heart's core."

TABLE OF CONTENTS

I will arise and go now, for always night and day
I hear lake water lapping with low sounds by the shore;
While I stand on the roadway, or on the pavements grey,
I hear it in the deep heart's core.

                    W.B. Yeats, "The Lake Isle of Innisfree"

AT THE EDGE

I.

Consolation

You brought me a tree from Hawaii, left it on the porch,
rooted in earthenware, heavy with fruit.
Later, I looked up from my desk to see
white petals gleam like pennants,
lashing leaves that surfed the wind,
a sound like uncooked rice being sifted and poured.
The light between the leaves was you,
restless with intelligence,
          quick   wild
stirring my heart at the borders of my splintered world.

At Nantasket

After you forgave me, we drank Cristal
from paper cups. The tide dragged in white caps
to spray the windshield and the lot with suds.
Gulls sought out sea clams tossed among the rocks
and dropped them on the tarmac from a height.

Your soft words circled mine like tidal pools,
their velocity dispelled. Fantasies
melted like thin rain gone to mist.
The sea had threatened but done nothing.
The enormity of what we had done silenced us.

I walked the shore in a fizzle of rain,
the rip-tide having left long tidal pools
            along the rippled flats.
I imagined how good the new us would be,
        how good we will be—
a little spent, but heady, like champagne.

Mid-Winter's Night Ballad

To lose you, at last, in anecdote or song—
I'd not expected we'd end this way.

To wear you like a pair of diamond earrings
or a red rose necklace. To dream no more.

Strange to be cool and sort of practical.

Goodbye, my funny Valentine,
my own fat-bottomed Cupid boy.
Your tales have served their time.
Tell them anew beside the fire.

It may be your last wounding,
like the willow branch of winter
holds me steady as a flute note,
keeps me strong enough to sing.

Colored Flowers and Tiny Messages

I wanted not to think of the way we hid the dark scar
of your grave
under coloured flowers and tiny messages.
What would I speak of on that bitter day—
not the weather or the trees unprepared for spring.
Everything we lost with you—
your bright stare, your serious smile, your graceless dancing
        beyond the last reach of our hopes.

I wanted not to think of you after we turned aside—you
left where neither leaves nor birdsong would ever reach you,
your only shelter the grey grass holding on to winter
        and your cold cover of flowers.

I Ask You

To create the sensibility by which I'm understood,
the way the Earth senses a new season,
I imagine knowing it before.
When did I know it before?
You say we have known it all along.

If at last I wander past the lament of the surf
into realms of pure beauty and kindness, I ask you
    What would that look like?

You walk ahead of me. I've been pursuing you
to ask about all this, and now that I am near,
      you have nothing to say.

"We have wandered into a place of pure beauty and kindness,
together," you say. "We are unfettered," you say.
     "Isn't that enough?"

On the Steps of the Met 1997

When the first wasp would not stop flying near me,
I sat still and let it stay. A yellow pest with thin legs,
it did not find my skin but entered the silver mouth
of the Diet Pepsi can, crawled inside and
        joined another in there.

I let those two fill themselves while
I finished my greasy knish and thought
how sad that you and I no longer wanted each other.

One wasp staggered out, flew off, then the other.
They were two cabs on their way in Manhattan.
Inside the Met, I found again what I love most:
that Vermeer portrait, the folds of the woman's scarf,
their deep shadows coming so close without touching.

Boston Common

I put on my reading glasses to help my ex-husband
do up the buttons on his leather gloves. I fumbled.
"What a pair we are," he said,
"me with my sore wrists, you with your weak thumbs,"

and off we went, two grandparents set
to march against the war in Ukraine,
he with his plastic knee,
I with my bad eyes,
waving each other on like old friends
where we'd met for so many marches over the years,
for peace for God's sake,
for peace on earth.

See What You've Missed

Cooking a nine-vegetable stew, remember
the way it was that Christmas Eve in the South End?
Now, cold potato soup alone in the suburbs.

What does it mean if I say this years later?

Listen, last night I was on a crying jag
when my neighbour Ethan banged on the door,
demanding to know if it's true
I have mice. I became my Aunt Barbara,
proud but piqued, pulling down my acting skills
to defend my little patch against aspersion.
I raised my voice to his. He wiped his eyes,
opened his hands, "Ok, Ok, just checking,
but I had to know. I'm so nervous," he said.
We cried together.

I wanted to run to where you are lying
and say, "Look, it's like the time
we fought about that velvet couch I hated
and wept on many a time after you got sick.
See what you've missed since you died?"

Crossing the Distance

My sister takes in dogs of all shapes and sizes
      but she does not take in me.

I call to her but no sound I make
is made of words that can cross the distance between us.

Last night she was just a cutout on a hill,
a pack of curs at her heels, the sky burning,
and I knew she did not belong to me.

II.

Midsummer Poetry Workshop, New York City

Gladioli double over from the hot winds. The gummy air glooms.
Across the road from Poets House, green benches face the water. I sit
and stare. What waves pull up on the riverbank all the way from Jersey,
thoughtful, cooling, detached—subtle colours of purest intent. The master
has tasked us to write Japanese poetry. I want to jump in the Hudson,
swim to the other side, see what happens. The water is the sky. Nothing.
Nothing informs. Nothing tells me. A sun-bleached fish lies dead in the
   golden debris.
I am in view of a rapturous creature. Birds stay away. They'll have to feed
in a lusher landscape. The air is fevered with dust like winter screaming itself
into a snowy rage. The goldfish is the map of love. Anything can happen.

> Against the brick wall
> I throw red clay cups.
> Noises will come back to me.

A Kind of Madness

I am going all the way now to Sligo,
to the call.
The path is straight.
I'll take the poet with me
and eat the local food.

I've used up the world I was given,
the stain of travel forever underfoot.
My walls ache with longing.

But I know in Sligo I'll be free
to follow ancestral voices.
What love is left for me
grows wild on Innisfree.
I am a mad heiress.

(June 13, 2015
150th birthday of W. B. Yeats)

Paris

Which roads did we chance upon in Paris that first day
  where the curb smoothed down onto cobblestones?
Back streets, centuries old, blocks of shops with empty
windows—
  You said, "Not shops, flats. People have gone to work."

At Le Drug Store, we ordered grilled cheese like WWII
Americans.
  I studied the menu. *Le Café Glace* must be iced coffee.
The waiter brought a black, frosted glass—no sugar, no ice, no
cream.
  I drank it anyway. It was excellent.

Drenching rain now; we returned to the street, headed for the
Tuileries.
  We looked for a bench to sit on—all taken.
A man stood under dripping trees renting rickety tin seats for deux
francs.
  On principle you refused to lease a chair.

We queued holding hands for the Musée d'Orsay,
  sweating hot in our raincoats. You said,
"Paris is so romantic. I want to stay forever
  because I'm with you." We had not laughed all day.

NYC Port Authority

The resident homeless talks to herself,
wearing all her outfits in layers.
She's become a cocoon for her voice
to drone from. She sits on the bathroom floor
against the damp wall, clasping black, bulging bags.
She holds an animated conversation
with the empty space. Something has angered her.
She argues until her head droops. She dozes.
She dozes as I did last night in my bed,
lamplight in my eyes, phone on the night stand,
glass of water, Tylenol, emergency numbers.

As I do, I snuggled in my warm blankets,
a book, let's say *The Best American* Something
slipping between my fingers.

Winslow Homer Exhibition

Love's declensions—yes, why, if only, free.
Down to March,
      regression
            waiting
                  pain.
Instead of letting go, I tried to drain
reviving drink from the foamed, tantrumed, sea.

April. Record crowds throng the MFA.
You'd gone with someone younger, so I thought
that's that, until I viewed the life he caught,
in broad meadows, seawater bays.

Later, Homer seemed splashed many places
around Boston—watery *Blue Boat* shots
blown up on posters less publicizing
than stealing the show. And wistful field boys' faces
blurred in ochers and forget-me-nots,
June's consolation smiling in their eyes.

La Danse

At the Pavilion on Tremont,
she is bewitched by *The Dance*,
steps practiced to thoughtlessness,
dancers covered though bare,
their expressions bright though blank.
They are scribbled thoughts.
They speak in perfect sentences.

She feels the undulations from the stage,
looks for a lapse, a fault, a misstep.
There are only silky turns,
      deliberate falls,
           full commands of the air.

III.

Nightcap

in memory of CFMM

Back from waitressing,
your midnight habit was to return home
for a cuppa strong tea without the milk
set aside for breakfast.

Child care experts would have frowned
at my late hours sipping a bitter adult cup
along with your sparkling confidences,
your pre-war Cambridge stories more real
to your first-born than they could have been
to the younger ones tucked up in bed.
Your heart opened; I stoked the coal fire.

Those nightcaps were our singular bond,
and though I've drunk milky, sugarless tea
for decades, I'll not be weaned off
that early tender brew.

45

in memory of APM

When I was tall enough to see
over the white formica table,
there they were, playing 45.
Big red hands, cut and gouged,
crumpled fingers, bitten nails
clutching cards to be slammed
on the table with thumps
and ah-hahs. A winner!
I, too, wanted the flushed face
from throwing down a Joker
or a five
on dark winter evenings.
Frank DiTullio, Billy Couming
and Daddy played
War, Old Maid, even 45 with me,
but I was ignorant
that gabbing was worse
than reneging at this grownup table.
So I hid out on the window sill
wrapped in a lace curtain
like an angel
peering out on a world
I could not understand.
The set of their jaws,
the tightened fists,
shouts of joy,
all of them holding their tricks.
The Angel Gabriel
could have dropped in

and blown his trumpet;
the Second Coming
could have come and gone.
They wouldn't have heard a thing.

My Life at 50

For the first 10 years,
I woke when my father shook me,
ate peanut butter toast for breakfast,
made friends on purpose,
wrote poems I hid among the pages
    of trash novels,
read the evening paper,
worked the crossword in my bath,
slept in bleached-out pyjamas, but
slept very deep.

For the last 10 years,
I have written mediocre poetry,
made friends by coincidence,
slept uneasy in my skin,
eaten well sometimes
from the sale of a clever sonnet,
and loved a man with big hands,
though not very well, he tells me,
not very well at all,
but well enough, I guess.

This Time of Night

Under the white coverlet, now as then,
the sweeping tide of the sheets,
the same cool turning. I dive, I tumble
    toward dreams.
Memories run wild. Night must have
released all its prisoners—
my ghosts are younger now.

I love this time of night. My bed makes me
alert to everything—the hours,
the planes in flight, the faucet drip.
My senses gleam like candles.

After Viewing the Dutch Masters

I've always liked the late afternoon light
and don't turn on the electric until six.
My sister says I live like Rembrandt
though it's hardly about melancholy.
I just like the way things look in air turning darker,
the rimming of objects from the setting sun,
life reduced to the elemental.

Every woman deserves one true moment of clarity,

       and this is mine—

this blur of shadows busy with details:
coats flung on the sofa back,
               cat stretching her full length,
                      the table laid for supper.
The late afternoon light.

After the Wake

After the wake, I went alone
to her house.
Nothing had changed:
pink, pilled slippers
beside the heating vent
on the bedroom floor,
bathrobe stuffed on top
of the radiator,
her face in a faded Polaroid
tucked inside the mirror frame.
An ashtray near the bride doll
on her chenille bedspread
should have depressed me,
but each impression
had its own spindrift,
tossing me one to the other.

Wallpaper roses invoked
her Revlon lipstick,
the watery blue of milk glass,
her eyes, of course.
"I'll come back to haunt you,"
she said, teasing the granddaughters
in her all-white nightgown.
"Nana, you look like a bride!"
sent her into spasms of laughter.

I paused to comb her dolly's hair,
but, no, work to do.
I shredded a lifetime of paper:
diplomas, prom favors,

thank-you notes,
Mass cards, photos,
gummy clippings,
gas bills, prescriptions,
letters from camp,
take-out menus,
wish lists, crosswords,
dictionary look-ups,
3-for-2 coupons,
warranties, Christmas bows,
wheels-on-meals plates
fell into a sack.
It weighed almost nothing.

They Are Present by Their Absence

I drift through spaces empty of the others,
the only sound a refrigerator's whirr.

Objects noticed when others aren't present—
the orangey smell from a Red Sox trash can,
laundry half-folded on the dining table.

I go to the TV room but don't turn on the set,
check out photos on the parents' night stand.

I wander back to my daughter's kitchen,
the fridge covered with pictures—
        first baseball uniform, first girlfriend,
        a first grader's apology, "I Sory Momy."

Paper napkins lie slack in their wooden holder.
Cheerios cling to the inside of bowls.

Sweater Break

Two days of determined rains were over.
My long-absent daughter showed up
to walk me through the neighbourhood.
The tall grasses at the end of the footpath
had at last crowned to my height.
We walked under trees,
limbs hanging lower, thicker, darker.
Everywhere I looked, I saw green freed.
Julie pointed out the losses and gains
    to the citified me.
The flowers had had a time of it,
petals dissolved into mulched carpets
    under the bushes.
She led me by the hand around soaked lawns,
schooled me on the climate's insult to wildlife.
I could sense her affections.

We needed sweaters but stayed outdoors,
afraid we would miss something.

Grandson

The family says he has a shadow
across his brow,
looks always to the side
as if, if he could turn his head
a bit further, he might see
what troubles him.
I know the steadiness of his arm,
the even sound of his step.
My hands know his smooth cheek, his jaw.

The Edge of Tears

My day begins in moonlight. I smell a wind shift
from somewhere lifting blades of grass,
skipping over stones, surrounding my heart.
I am so glad of this.
Let us shelter in anticipation of lightning.
Come with me to the edge of tears
where candles gutter but stay lit.
My head is bursting with flowers.

ACKNOWLEDGMENTS

I could not have produced this humble collection without the many poets who live in and around the Boston/Cambridge metro area.

I've mentioned elsewhere two teachers whose patience, kindness, and insight have helped my writing grow and evolve in years of writing workshops: Tom Daley and Katia Kapovich. Tom is also leader of the wonderful monthly Boston Poetry Salon, where featured poets read and discuss their work. An Open Mic follows. Sitting in those rooms have been poet-friends Emily Axelrod, Alec Solomita, and Mary Beth Hines, whose astute suggestions have often made the difference in my work. Add to them the enduring presence of Carl Slater, my former husband, who has spent untold hours on the phone with me reading favourite poems. I am thankful for the Zoom screens that have kept all of us together since 2020, introducing a number of writers who live at a distance.

In Hingham, MA, where I make my home, I've gathered many times with poetry lovers during National Poetry Month, immersed in volumes of the greats, e.g., W.B. Yeats and Emily Dickinson, along with poets in brilliant collections like *African American Poetry: 250 Years of Struggle & Song* by the *New Yorker* editor, Kevin Young. These educational sessions have been conducted in the parlor of the Old Ship Church Parish House by Rev. Ken Read-Brown and Hingham Poet Laureate, Elizabeth Torrey. Their enormous effort for months beforehand has given us interesting information and endless pleasure.

Abiding gratitude is sent to all of the above as well as to London friends Anne-Marie Fyfe and Cahal Dallat; Caroline Bracken of Bray, Ireland; and Aidan Rooney from Hingham, MA. To my daughter Julie, my college-aged grandchildren, Mia and Sean, my friends of many years, thank you for your support with special gratitude to Kathleen Regan.

ABOUT THE AUTHOR

Gail Moran Slater is one of five generations of her family born in Boston, MA, the result of a diaspora created by the Great Hunger of 1847 in Ireland. She grew up in Boston, attending public and private schools, and trained to be a teacher at Boston State College, now known as the University of Massachusetts/Boston. She earned a Master's degree in English Education from Boston University. After a career in education, she worked in business until 2009 (at Idearc, formerly Verizon Yellow Pages), then returned to the classroom as a Teacher of ESL to adults. She lives south of Boston in a beautiful New England town, Hingham, MA. a place mad for poetry. She has a wonderful daughter and two amazing college-age grandchildren.

This book is set in Garamond Premier Pro, which originated in 1988 when type-designer Robert Slimbach visited the Plantin-Moretus Museum in Antwerp, Belgium, to study its collection of Claude Garamond's metal punches and typefaces. During the 1500s Garamond—a Parisian punch-cutter—produced a refined array of book types that combined an unprecedented degree of balance and elegance, for centuries standing as the pinnacle of beauty and practicality in typefounding. They were based on the handwriting of Angelo Vergecio, court librarian of the French king, Francis I. Slimbach has created a new interpretation based on Garamond's designs and on compatible italics cut by Robert Granjon, Garamond's contemporary.

Copies of this book are available
at all bookstores including Amazon
and can be ordered directly
from Gail Moran Slater
2704 Hockley Dr.
Hingham, MA 02043
Send $15 per book
plus $4 shipping
by check payable
to Gail Moran Slater.

•

For more information on the work of Gail Moran Slater
visit www.antrimhousebooks.com/authors.html.
The author can be contacted at
gailslater@verizon.net

CPSIA information can be obtained
at www.ICGtesting.com
Printed in the USA
BVHW041216310323
661520BV00006B/413

9 798986 552255